Learn all the key facts with CGP!

Want to remember all the crucial facts for OCR GCSE Computer Science?
This CGP Knowledge Organiser is here to help!

We've condensed every topic down to the vital definitions, facts and diagrams, making it all easy to memorise.

To check you've really got your facts straight, there's also a matching Knowledge Retriever book that'll test you on every page.

CGP — still the best! ☺

Our sole aim here at CGP is to produce the highest quality books — carefully written, immaculately presented and dangerously close to being funny.

Then we work our socks off to get them out to you — at the cheapest possible prices.

Contents

Section Seven — Design, Testing and IDEs

Published by CGP.
Based on the classic CGP style created by Richard Parsons.

Editors: Martha Bozic, Michael Bushell, Shaun Harrogate, Andy Hurst.

With thanks to Sammy El-Bahrawy and Shaun Whorton for the proofreading.
With thanks to Alice Dent for the copyright research.

ISBN: 978 1 78908 949 3

Exam Reference Language OCR April 2020. OCR maintains the current version of the Exam Reference Language and specification on the OCR website. You should always check for the latest version and any updates. (https://www.ocr.org.uk/qualifications/gcse/computer-science-j277-from-2020/)

Printed by Elanders Ltd, Newcastle upon Tyne.
Clipart from Corel®

Computer Systems and The CPU

Computer Systems

HARDWARE — the physical stuff in a computer system, e.g. keyboard, CPU, etc.

SOFTWARE — the programs that a computer system runs, e.g. operating system, games, web browser, etc.

EMBEDDED SYSTEMS — computers built into other devices, usually as control systems. E.g. they could control:

Dishwashers

Microwaves

Sat navs

They're usually **easier** to design, **cheaper** to produce, and more **efficient** at their task than general purpose systems.

External pieces of hardware like a keyboard or mouse are called peripherals.

Four Common CPU Components

CENTRAL PROCESSING UNIT (CPU)

— where a computer processes all data and instructions.

1. **Control Unit (CU)** — controls the flow of data in and out of the CPU. Manages the fetching, decoding and execution of instructions.

2. **Arithmetic Logic Unit (ALU)** — does calculations including addition, subtraction, multiplication and division. Also performs binary shifts and logic operations.

3. **Cache** — stores regularly used data for quick access. Low capacity and expensive. There are three levels of cache memory:

L1 → L2 → L3

Decreasing speed, increasing capacity

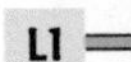
4. **Registers** — temporarily hold small amounts of data. They're extremely fast to read/write to.

Three Factors Affecting CPU Performance

1. **Number of cores** — each core processes data independently, so more cores means more instructions can be carried out per second. Some software is designed to take advantage of multicore processing.

2. **Clock speed** — the number of instructions a single processor core can carry out per second.

3. **Cache size** — a larger CPU cache gives the CPU faster access to more data.

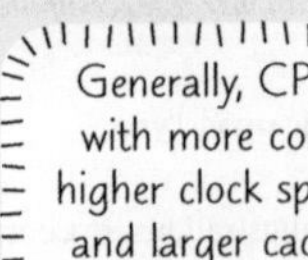
Generally, CPUs with more cores, higher clock speeds and larger caches will have better performance, but cost more.

How The CPU Works

Von Neumann Architecture

In the Von Neumann architecture, data and instructions are both stored in the same memory.

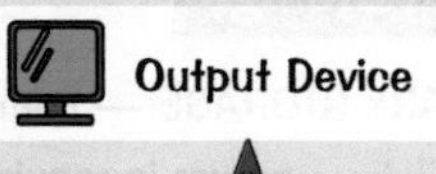

Central Processing Unit (CPU)

Control Unit

Program Counter (PC) — holds the memory address of the instruction for each cycle.

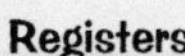

Registers

Memory Address Register (MAR) — holds any memory address about to be used by the CPU. The address could point to data or an instruction.

Arithmetic Logic Unit

Accumulator — stores intermediate results of calculations in the ALU.

Memory Data Register (MDR) — holds the actual data or instruction, either fetched from memory or waiting to be written to memory.

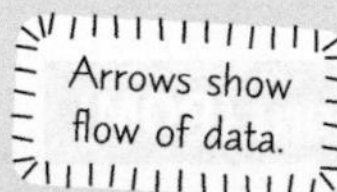

Memory — holds program instructions and data.

Fetch-Execute Cycle

The fetch-execute cycle repeats continuously while the computer is running.

1 FETCH

- Memory address copied from the program counter to the MAR.
- Instruction copied from memory to the MDR.
- Program counter incremented to point to the next instruction.

2 DECODE

- Instruction in the MDR decoded by the control unit.
- Control unit prepares for next step, e.g. by loading values into the MAR or MDR.

3 EXECUTE

Decoded instruction carried out. Examples of instructions:

- Load data from memory.
- Write data to memory.
- Do calculation or logic operation (using the ALU).

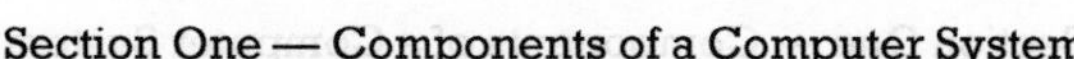

Memory

Primary Storage

PRIMARY STORAGE — memory that the CPU can read/write to quickly, e.g. RAM.

VOLATILE — power is required for the component to retain data.

NON-VOLATILE — the component retains data even when the power is turned off.

Random Access Memory (RAM)

RAM — the main temporary memory in a computer.

Volatile memory.

Can be read from and written to.

Programs and files are copied here from secondary storage while in use.

Slower than the CPU cache, but faster than secondary storage.

Virtual Memory

RAM can fill up if too many apps, or memory-intensive apps, are running, so some data is moved to a location in secondary storage called virtual memory.

This data is moved back to RAM when the CPU needs it. Data transfer is slower on secondary storage, so this slows the computer's performance.

Read Only Memory (ROM)

ROM — the main permanent memory in a computer.

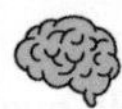

Non-volatile memory.

Can only be read from, not written to.

Small amount of memory built into the motherboard.

Contains BIOS (Basic Input Output System) — instructions needed for the computer to boot up.

ROM is read only, but it is possible to update the BIOS on a ROM chip.

Secondary Storage

Two Types of Internal Storage

SECONDARY STORAGE — non-volatile storage where programs and data are kept for later use.

Hard Disk Drives (HDDs)

- Moving parts.
- Store data magnetically on metal disks.
- Can be noisy.

Solid State Drives (SSDs)

- No moving parts.
- Use flash memory for faster read/write times.
- Usually quiet/silent.

Four Types of External Storage

1. **Flash drives & memory cards** — solid state storage used to expand the capacity of small devices.

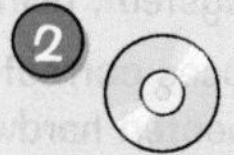

2. **Optical discs** — e.g. CDs. Can be read-only, write-once or rewritable.

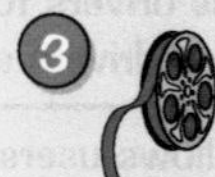

3. **Magnetic tape** — used by organisations to store huge amounts of data.

4. **External HDDs & SSDs** — portable versions of internal storage. Often used for backups.

Comparing Storage Types

Optical Disc → Memory Card → Magnetic Tape → HDD → SSD

Average Read/Write Speed

Optical Disc → Memory Card → SSD → HDD → Magnetic Tape

Average Capacity

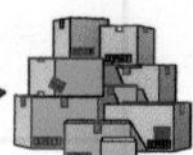

Magnetic Tape → Optical Disc → HDD → Memory Card → SSD

Average Cost (per GB)

	Internal HDD	Internal SSD	Memory Card	Optical Disc	Magnetic Tape
Portability	Low	Low	High	High	High
Durability and Reliability	Damaged by impacts. Long read/ write life.	Shock resistant. Limited rewrites.	Shock resistant. Limited rewrites.	Easily scratched. Limited rewrites. Suitable long term storage.	Damaged by impacts, heat and magnets. Suitable long term storage.

System Software — The OS

Five Functions of an Operating System (OS)

Function	Features
1 Peripheral management and drivers	• Communicates with internal hardware, and peripherals connected to the system, using drivers. • Chooses correct drivers for connected hardware on startup. • Installs drivers for new hardware and updates drivers automatically. I think you've got the wrong driver...
2 Providing a user interface	12:00 Allows users to interact with a computer. Different interfaces are designed for different types of user: • Graphical User Interfaces (GUIs) have windows, icons, menus and pointers. Designed for everyday users. • Command-Line Interfaces are text-based and use fewer system resources than GUIs. Used by advanced users.
3 Memory management and multitasking	• Moves application data to main memory when in use and removes it when it's no longer needed. • Allocates memory addresses so apps don't overwrite or interfere with each other. • Divides CPU processing time between tasks to complete them efficiently. • Uses memory buffers to store data until other components or processes are ready. These all help the CPU to multitask.
4 File and disk management	TXT MP3 JPEG HTML The OS uses extensions to match files with apps. • Organises files into a hierarchical structure of folders. • Deals with naming, saving, moving, editing and deleting files and folders. • Splits the hard disk into sectors and decides where files are written to. • Maintains the hard disk with utility software.
5 User management	• Controls which users, and how many users, can access the computer system. • Grants users access to specific data and resources — e.g. their own personal data and account, but not that of other users. • Uses anti-theft measures to prevent access for other users — e.g. password or pin protection.

System Software — Utilities

Defragmentation Software

UTILITY SOFTWARE — software designed to help maintain a computer system.

Defragmentation software reorganises a HDD by putting related data back together. This speeds up reading/writing files as the read/write head no longer has to move as much.

SSDs don't need to be defragmented, they can access fragmented files quickly.

1 **Files are stored in available spaces on the hard disk.**

2 **As they're moved, deleted, or change size, small gaps appear on the disk.**

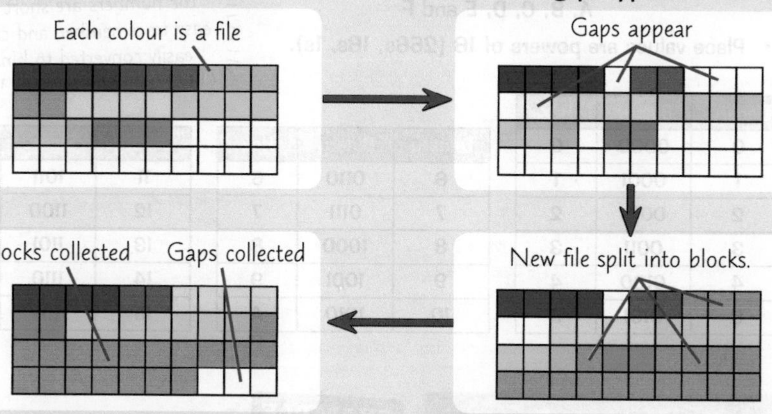

3 **When writing new files to the disk, the OS splits them into smaller blocks to fill the gaps.**

4 **Defragmentation software puts the fragmented files back together. It also groups free space to prevent further fragmentation.**

Compression Software

Reduces size of files by permanently or temporarily removing data from them.

Compressed files take up less disk space and are quicker to upload and download.

Compressed files need to be extracted before they can be used.

Encryption Software

Scrambles (encrypts) data to stop third-parties from accessing it.

To decrypt it back to its original form, a special 'key' is needed.

Only the computers of intended readers have the key, so stolen encrypted data is still secure.

Strong encryption makes it almost impossible to find the key through brute force methods.

Number Systems

Three Important Number Systems

1 DENARY (BASE 10)
- Ten digits: 0, 1, 2, 3, 4, 5, 6, 7, 8 and 9
- Place values are powers of 10 (100s, 10s, 1s).

2 BINARY (BASE 2)
- Two digits: 0 and 1
- Place values are powers of 2 (8s, 4s, 2s, 1s).

3 HEXADECIMAL (BASE 16)
- Sixteen digits: 0, 1, 2, 3, 4, 5, 6, 7, 8, 9, A, B, C, D, E and F
- Place values are powers of 16 (256s, 16s, 1s).

Programmers like hex because the numbers are short and easy to remember, and can be easily converted to binary.

Denary	Binary	Hex
0	0000	0
1	0001	1
2	0010	2
3	0011	3
4	0100	4
5	0101	5

Denary	Binary	Hex
6	0110	6
7	0111	7
8	1000	8
9	1001	9
10	1010	A

Denary	Binary	Hex
11	1011	B
12	1100	C
13	1101	D
14	1110	E
15	1111	F

Converting Binary to Denary...

1. Put the number in a binary place value table.
2. Add up the place values in columns where there's a 1.

EXAMPLE

Convert 10011100 from binary to denary.

1

128	64	32	16	8	4	2	1
1	0	0	1	1	1	0	0

2 128 + 16 + 8 + 4 = 156

...and Denary to Binary

1. Draw a binary place value table.
2. Keep subtracting the biggest place values you can until you're left with 0.
3. If you subtracted a place value, put a 1 in that column, otherwise put a 0.

EXAMPLE

Convert 170 from denary to binary.

1

128	64	32	16	8	4	2	1

2 170 – 128 = 42
42 – 32 = 10
10 – 8 = 2
2 – 2 = 0

3

128	64	32	16	8	4	2	1
1	0	1	0	1	0	1	0

Converting Hexadecimal

Converting Hex to Denary...

1. Put the number in a hex place value table.
2. Multiply (in denary) the values in each column.
3. Add up the results.

EXAMPLE

Convert A2 from hexadecimal to denary.

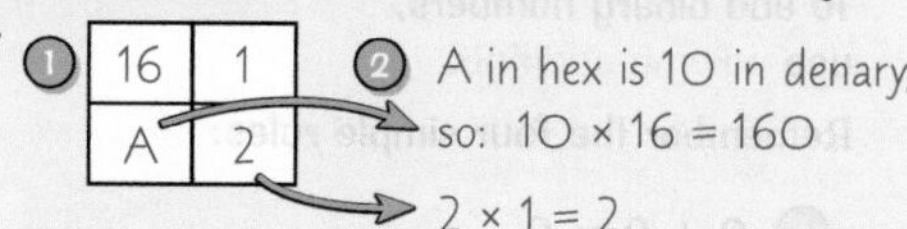

①

16	1
A	2

② A in hex is 10 in denary, so: 10 × 16 = 160

2 × 1 = 2

③ A2 is 160 + 2 = 162 in denary.

...and Denary to Hex

1. Divide by 16 to get a quotient and a remainder.
2. Convert each value to hex.
3. The quotient is the 1st digit and the remainder is the 2nd.

EXAMPLE

Convert 43 from denary to hexadecimal.

① 43 ÷ 16 = 2 remainder 11

② 2 in denary is 2 in hex. 11 in denary is B in hex.

③ 43 is 2B in hexadecimal.

Converting Binary to Hex...

1. Put the number in a table that repeats 8, 4, 2, 1, ... Add zeros to the front so that it splits into nibbles.
2. For each nibble, add up the place values in columns where there's a 1, and convert into hex.

EXAMPLE

Convert 110 1101 from binary to hex.

①

8	4	2	1	8	4	2	1
0	1	1	0	1	1	0	1

② 4 + 2 = 6
6 in denary is 6 in hex.

8 + 4 + 1 = 13
13 in denary is D in hex.

So 110 1101 is 6D in hexadecimal.

...and Hex to Binary

1. Convert each hex digit into a 4-bit binary number.
2. Put the nibbles together.

EXAMPLE

Convert E4 from hexadecimal to binary.

① E in hex is 14 in denary, which is 1110 in binary.
4 in hex is 4 in denary, which is 0100 in binary.

② So E4 is 1110 0100 in binary.

Using Binary

Binary Addition

To add binary numbers, use column addition.

Remember the four simple rules:

1. 0 + 0 = 0
2. 0 + 1 = 1
3. 1 + 1 = 10 (carry a 1)
4. 1 + 1 + 1 = 11 (carry a 1)

EXAMPLE

Work out 10101010 + 111011.

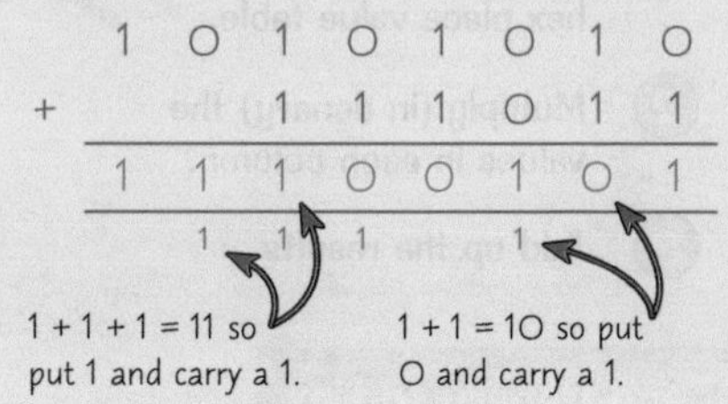

1 + 1 + 1 = 11 so put 1 and carry a 1.

1 + 1 = 10 so put 0 and carry a 1.

Binary Shifts

BINARY SHIFT — move every bit in a binary number left or right a certain number of places.

Gaps at the beginning or end of the number are filled in with 0s.

Left shifts MULTIPLY.
For every place shifted left, the number is doubled.

Right shifts DIVIDE.
For every place shifted right, the number is halved.

Overflow Errors

OVERFLOW ERROR — when binary arithmetic gives a result that requires more bits than the CPU is expecting.

Overflow errors can lead to a loss of data or precision.

- In binary addition, two 8-bit numbers might add to give a 9-bit number. If the CPU expects an 8-bit answer then bits will be lost.
- Left shifts can cause the most significant bits to be lost.
- Right shifts can cause the least significant bits to be lost.

The most significant bit is the left-most bit. The least significant bit is the right-most bit.

EXAMPLE

Describe the effect of a 2-place left shift on 01011101.

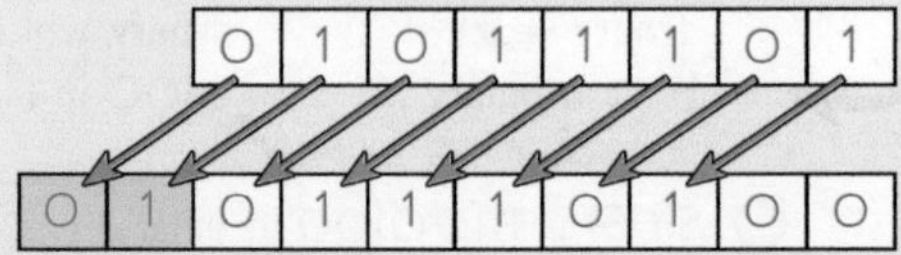

The number has been doubled twice, or multiplied by $2^2 = 4$.

If there are only 8 bits available to store the result, then the two most significant bits will overflow.

Units and Compression

Eight Units of Data Size

Computers can only store and process binary data.

They use 1s and 0s to represent the flow of electricity — a 1 shows that electricity is flowing, and a 0 shows that it isn't flowing.

Each 1 or 0 in binary data is a bit (<u>b</u>inary dig<u>it</u>). The size of a file is the number of 1s and 0s that make up its data.

Traditionally, each unit is defined to be 1024 times bigger than the previous one.

Name	Size
1 Bit (b)	A single binary digit (1 or 0)
2 Nibble	4 bits
3 Byte (B)	8 bits
4 Kilobyte (kB)	1000 bytes
5 Megabyte (MB)	1000 kilobytes
6 Gigabyte (GB)	1000 megabytes
7 Terabyte (TB)	1000 gigabytes
8 Petabyte (PB)	1000 terabytes

Data Compression

DATA COMPRESSION — making file sizes smaller, while trying to stay as true to the original as possible.

Benefits of data compression:

- Compressed files use less storage space.
- Streaming/downloading compressed files takes less bandwidth.
- Some services like email have file size limits — compression can get a file below the limit.

Two Types of Compression

1. LOSSY COMPRESSION — permanently removes data from the file.
2. LOSSLESS COMPRESSION — temporarily removes data to store the file, and restores it to its original state when opened.

	Pros	Cons
Lossy	• Big reduction in file size, so they can be stored easier, and downloaded faster. • Commonly used — lots of software can read lossy files.	• Loses data — the file can't be turned back into the original. • Can't be used on text/software. • Reduction in quality.
Lossless	• No reduction in quality. • File can be turned back into the original. • Can be used on text/software.	• Comparatively small reduction in file size — lossless files take up more storage space than lossy files.

Characters

Character Sets

CHARACTERS — uppercase and lowercase letters, the digits 0-9, and symbols like ?, + and £. Used to make words and strings.

CHARACTER SETS — collections of characters that a computer recognises from their binary representation, used to convert characters to binary code and vice versa.

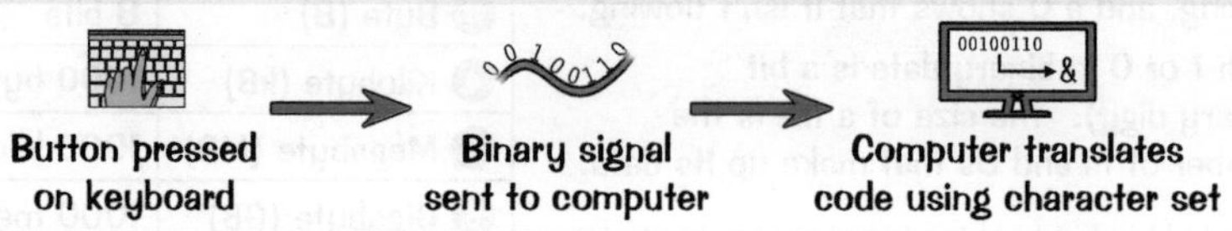

Two Important Character Sets

1 ASCII

- **Each character is given a 7-bit binary code — so ASCII can represent 128 different characters.**
- **An extra bit (0) is added to the start of each binary code so each character uses 1 byte.**
- **The codes for numbers and letters are ordered (A comes before B comes before C...).**

Character	Binary	Denary
A	0100 0001	65
B	0100 0010	66
C	0100 0011	67
a	0110 0001	97
b	0110 0010	98
c	0110 0011	99

As the codes are ordered, you can work out the code for one letter, given the code of another.

2 UNICODE®

- **Covers all major languages, including ones that use different alphabets, like Greek, Russian and Chinese.**
- **Uses multiple bytes for each character.**
- **The first 128 characters in Unicode® are the same as ASCII.**

Text File Sizes

File size (in bits) = number of bits per character × number of characters

EXAMPLE

How many bits would be needed to store "I'm a string, store me!" in 8-bit ASCII?

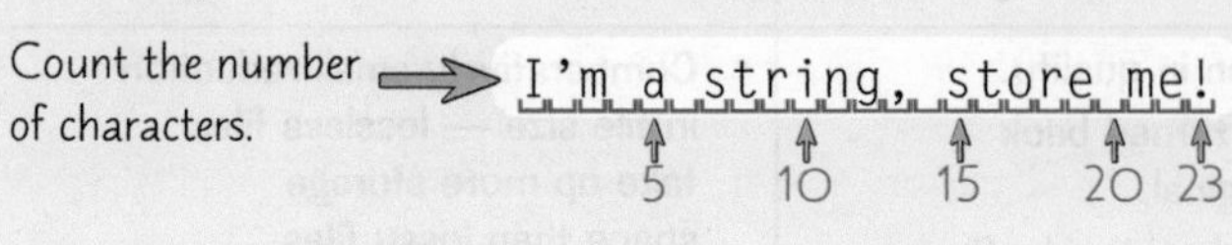

Use the formula. File size = 8 × 23 = 184 bits

Remember to count characters like spaces and symbols.

Storing Images

Representing Images

BITMAP — a type of image made up of lots of tiny dots, called pixels. The colour of each pixel is stored using a binary code.

IMAGE RESOLUTION — the number of pixels in a bitmap image. Often given as 'width × height'.

COLOUR DEPTH — the number of bits used to represent each pixel.

The number of colours that can be used for a given colour depth follows this formula:

Total number of colours = 2^n (where n = colour depth)

Colour depth = 2 bits

- Number of colours = 2^2 = 4
- In this example, 00 → white, 01 → light grey, 10 → dark grey, 11 → black.

11	01	10	00
01	10	00	10
10	00	10	01
00	10	01	11

Image File Sizes

Use this formula to calculate file size:

File size (in bits)
= image resolution × colour depth
= width × height × colour depth

Increasing the image resolution or colour depth will usually give a higher quality image, but a larger file size.

Calculate the size in kB of a 100 × 100 pixel image with a colour depth of 16 bits.

File size = 100 × 100 × 16
= 160 000 bits

160 000 bits
= 160 000 ÷ 8 = 20 000 bytes
= 20 000 ÷ 1000 = 20 kB

Metadata

METADATA — data stored in a file which contains information about the file. Helps the computer to recreate the image on screen from the binary data in each pixel.

Examples of metadata

- height & width
- colour depth
- resolution
- file format
- date created
- date last edited

Storing Sound

Key Definitions

SAMPLING	Converting an analogue sound wave into digital data that can be read and stored by a computer.
SAMPLE RATE	The number of samples taken per second. Usually measured in hertz (Hz). Also called sampling frequency.
BIT DEPTH	The number of bits available for each sample.

Sound Sampling Process

1. The amplitude of the sound wave is measured at fixed intervals, based on the sample rate. The measurements are only able to take certain values, based on the bit depth.

2. The sound is recreated digitally based on the measurements taken. It will be a similar shape to the analogue wave, but will have lost some accuracy.

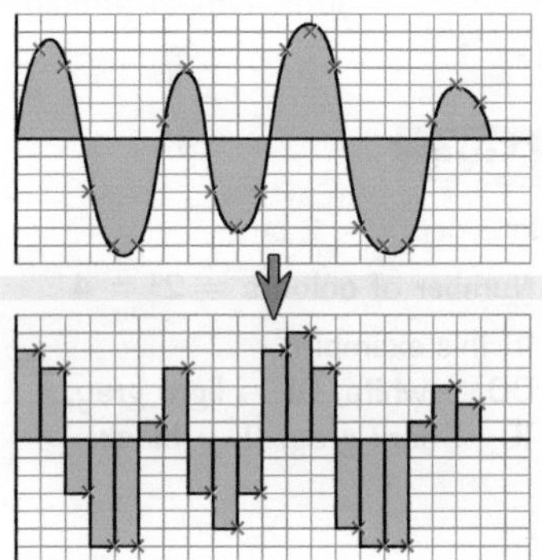

Sound File Sizes

File size (in bits) = Sample rate (in Hz) × bit depth × length (in seconds)

A higher sample rate or bit depth will give a higher quality sound file, but will increase the file size.

Couldn't agree more...

EXAMPLE

Calculate the file size in MB of a 50 second audio recording with a sample rate of 40 kHz and a bit depth of 8 bits.

1 kHz = 1000 Hz 40 kHz = 40 000 Hz

Use the formula. File size = 40 000 × 8 × 50 = 16 000 000 bits

Convert from bits to MB. 16 000 000 bits = 2 000 000 bytes
= 2000 kB = 2 MB

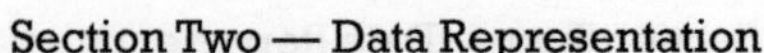

Types of Network

LANs — Local Area Networks

LANs cover small geographical areas at single sites — e.g. in businesses or schools.

LAN hardware is usually owned by the organisation using it.

They can be wired or wireless.

Users on a LAN can:

- Access and share files on the network.
- Share hardware.
- Share an Internet connection.
- Log in from any device on the network.
- Roll out security and software updates to all computers at once.

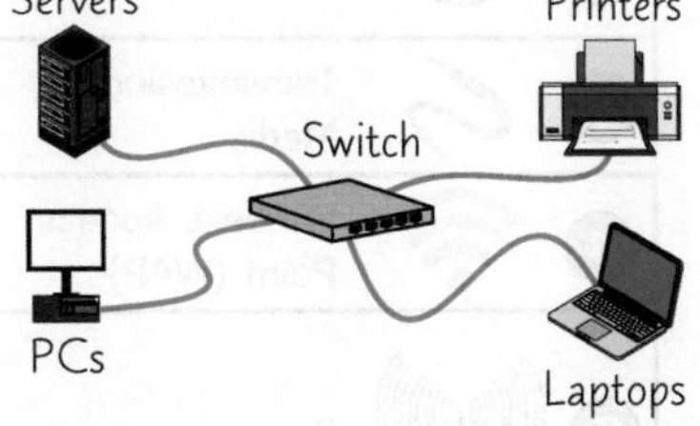

WANs — Wide Area Networks

WANs connect LANs in different geographical locations.

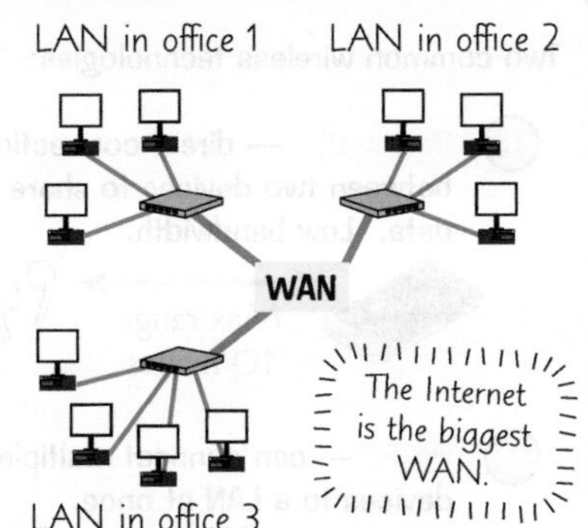

Organisations hire infrastructure (e.g. fibre optic lines or satellite links) from telecommunications companies, who own and manage the WAN.

More expensive to set up than LANs.

Network Performance

BANDWIDTH — amount of data that can be transferred in a given time. It's shared between devices on a network. Low bandwidth, heavy use (e.g. streaming video), or too many devices can slow a network.

Wired network performance can depend on the type of cables used.

Wireless performance depends on signal quality, which is affected by:

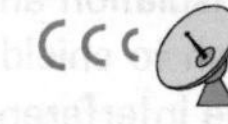
Range of the device

Interference from other networks

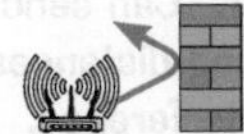
Physical obstructions

Network Hardware

Five Pieces of Network Hardware

Hardware	Function
1 Network Interface Controller (NIC)	Allows devices to connect to a network — usually built into the motherboard.
2 Switch	Receives and transmits data between devices on a LAN using MAC addresses.
3 Transmission Media	Wires or wireless radio waves that allow data transmission between devices.
4 Wireless Access Point (WAP)	Allows devices to connect to a network wirelessly. Similar to a switch.
5 Router	Transmits data between networks by directing data as 'packets' to their destination. Most 'routers' are a router, switch and WAP all in one.

Wired Networks

Three cables to connect devices on an Ethernet (wired) network:

1. Twisted pair — copper wires twisted together in pairs to reduce internal interference.
2. Coaxial — a single copper wire surrounded by plastic insulation and metallic mesh to shield from outside interference.

3. Fibre optic — transmits data as light. Can send data over long distances with little interference. High performance but expensive.

Wired networks tend to be faster and more reliable than wireless networks.

Wireless Networks

Radio waves transmit data between devices on wireless networks.

Two common wireless technologies:

1. Bluetooth® — direct connection between two devices to share data. Low bandwidth.

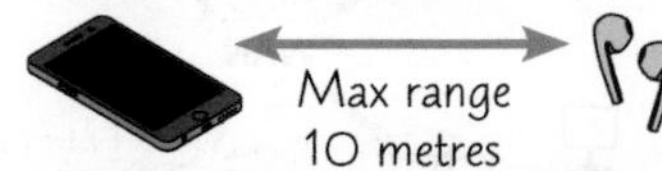

2. Wi-Fi® — can connect multiple devices to a LAN at once. High bandwidth.

Max range 40-100 metres

Wireless networks tend to be cheaper and more convenient than wired networks.

Networks and Topologies

Client-Server Networks

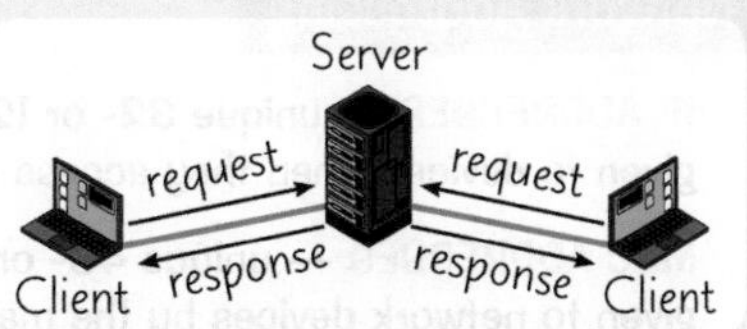

Files, software, user profiles and passwords are all stored centrally on the server.

Client sends a request to the server. Server processes the request and responds.

PROS

- **Easy file tracking — all stored centrally.**
- **Back up files and update software easily.**
- **Servers are reliable and always on.**
- **Security — servers can request passwords or access levels before fulfilling requests.**

CONS

- **Expensive to set up and maintain.**
- **If the server goes down all clients lose access.**
- **Servers can get overloaded with too many requests.**

Peer-to-Peer Networks

Devices connect directly — no server.

Files are stored on individual devices and shared with others.

PROS

- **Easy to maintain without expertise.**
- **No dependance on a server.**

CONS

- **Updates and backups are complicated.**
- **Hard to track files — copying between devices creates duplicates.**
- **Data could be lost if one device fails.**

Star Topology

All devices connect to a central switch or server that controls the network.

PROS

- **Network unaffected if a device fails.**
- **Easy to add more devices.**
- **High performance.**

CONS

- **Expensive for wired networks.**
- **Switch is a single point of failure.**

Mesh Topology

No switch — data sent along fastest route from one device to another.

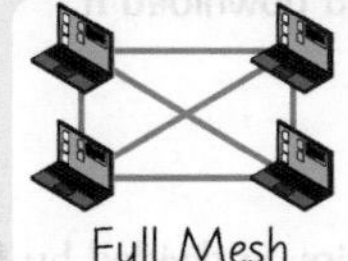

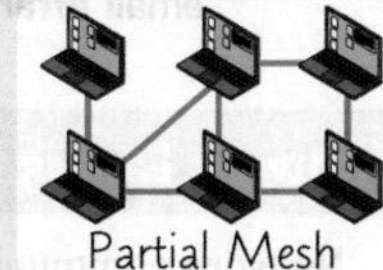

PROS

- **No single point of failure.**
- **Add devices without affecting performance.**

CONS

- **Expensive for wired networks.**
- **Hard to maintain lots of connections.**

Network Protocols

Network Addressing

IP ADDRESSES — unique 32- or 128-bit identifiers given to devices when they access a network.

E.g. 37.153.62.136 — denary

MAC ADDRESSES — unique 48- or 64-bit identifiers given to network devices by the manufacturer.

E.g. 98-81-55-CD-F2-2F — hex

Protocols

NETWORK STANDARD — a set of agreed requirements for hardware and software that allows different manufacturers to make compatible products.

NETWORK COMMUNICATION PROTOCOL — rules for how devices communicate, and how data is organised and transmitted across a network.

Transmission Control Protocol (TCP) — sets rules for how devices connect to a network. Splits and reassembles data packets. Checks they're sent and delivered.

Internet Protocol (IP) — directs packets to their destination across a network.

Simple Mail Transfer Protocol (SMTP) — sends and transfers emails between servers.

Post Office Protocol (POP) — retrieves emails from a server. Server deletes the email after you download it.

Hyper Text Transfer Protocol (HTTP) — web browsers use it to access websites and web servers.

HTTP Secure (HTTPS) — encrypts website information sent and received for security.

File Transfer Protocol (FTP) — accesses, edits and moves files between devices on a network.

Instant Messaging Access Protocol (IMAP) — retrieves emails from a server. Server holds it until you delete it.

Network Layers

Network communication is divided by functionality into layers.

Each layer is self-contained. It serves the layer above it and depends on all the layers below it.

Layer	Protocol
4	HTTP
3	TCP
2	IP
1	Ethernet

Benefits of network layers:

- Developers can each focus on one area of the network.
- Layers can be changed without affecting others.
- Standards develop ensuring compatibility between different pieces of hardware and software.

Internet Services

The Internet

INTERNET — a worldwide collection of computer networks.

WORLD WIDE WEB — a collection of websites hosted on web servers. Accessed through the http protocol.

URLs — addresses used to access web servers and resources on them, e.g:

https://www.cgpbooks.co.uk/guestbook

- Protocol: https://
- Domain name: www.cgpbooks.co.uk
- Path to a file or page: /guestbook

Domain Name Service (DNS)

A service made of many domain name servers that store domain names and matching IP addresses.

1. **Browser sends URL to DNS.**
2. **DNS finds matching IP address and sends it back to browser.**
3. **Browser requests web page from the web server at the IP address.**
4. **Web server processes the request and sends the web page back.**

Hosting and The Cloud

HOSTING — when a business uses its servers to store files for another organisation, e.g. hosting websites on web servers or files on file servers.

THE CLOUD — servers accessed over the Internet that offer a range of services including:

1. **Storing and accessing data and files — users need less storage space on their own computer.**
2. **Running cloud applications — users can access software without needing it on their own computer.**
3. **Providing increased processing power — users don't need to have expensive hardware in their computer.**

Pros of the cloud	Cons of the cloud
Access files from any device.	Requires Internet connection.
Easy to increase storage space.	Relies on host for security and backups.
No need for expensive hardware and the staff to manage it.	Stored data can be vulnerable to hackers.
Host provides security and backups.	Unclear who has ownership of data.
Automatic updates.	Expensive subscription fees.

Network Security Threats

Four Types of Network Attack

Attack	How it works
1 Data interception and theft	Sensitive information travelling on a network is intercepted using monitoring hardware and software like packet sniffers.
2 Brute-force	Automated software is used to try millions of potential passwords until one works.
3 Denial of service (DoS)	Hacker prevents users from accessing a network or website by flooding it with useless traffic/requests.
4 SQL injection	SQL code is typed into input boxes on a website. If the site doesn't have strong input validation, the hacker can gain access to databases behind the website. E.g. databases of customer details.

Malware

MALWARE — software designed to damage or disrupt a device or network.

Spyware — monitors user actions and sends info to the hacker.

Scareware — tricks user into paying to fix fake problems.

Ransomware — encrypts files. User pays for decryption key.

Rootkit — gives hackers admin access to the system.

Viruses — attached to other files. Only run or replicate when the file is opened.

Worms — like viruses but self-replicate so spread quickly.

Trojans — malware disguised as legitimate software. Do not replicate themselves.

Two Types of Social Engineering

SOCIAL ENGINEERING — gaining access to networks or sensitive information by using people as a system's weak point.

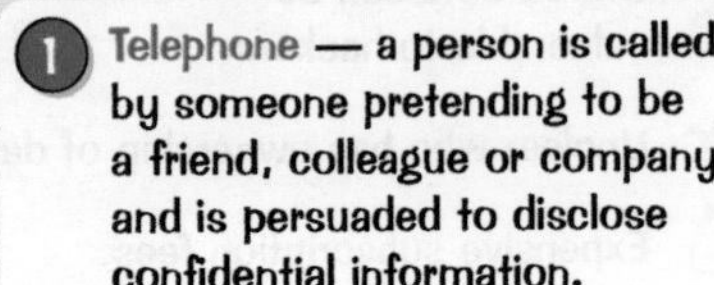

1 Telephone — a person is called by someone pretending to be a friend, colleague or company and is persuaded to disclose confidential information.

2 Phishing — criminals send emails pretending to be well-known businesses. They contain links to fake websites that ask users to update their personal information, which the criminals steal.

Network Security Measures

Passwords

Passwords prevent unauthorised users from accessing a network.

They should be strong and changed regularly to protect against brute-force attacks.

bossman ✗ Weak

B9£l@sTr!y*A  Strong

Encryption

Data is translated into a code that needs a specific decryption key to access.

Secures data sent over a network which limits the effectiveness of data interception attacks.

Secures data stored on the network which limits the effectiveness of SQL injection.

User Access Levels

User access levels can control:

- who has access to sensitive data,
- who has read/write access to files,
- who can change access levels of other users.

Limiting the number of people who can access sensitive data and important files makes social engineering and malware attacks less effective.

Anti-Malware Software

Anti-malware software prevents malware from damaging a network and the devices on it.

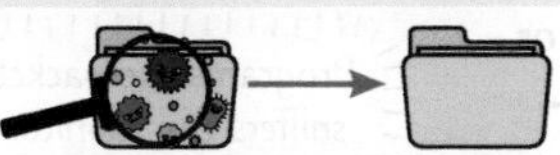

Antivirus programs isolate and destroy computer viruses.

Firewalls

Firewalls examine all data entering and leaving a network. They identify threats using a set of security rules, blocking unauthorised access and unwanted data.

Help to protect against most types of attack including brute-force, denial of service, malware and phishing.

Physical Security

Protects physical parts of a network from damage (e.g. theft and vandalism).

Locks and passcodes restrict access to areas like server rooms.

Surveillance equipment can deter intruders.

Penetration Testing

Organisations hire specialists to simulate attacks — they identify and report weaknesses in a network's security. The weaknesses can be fixed to help to protect against real network attacks.

Privacy and Ethical Issues

Privacy

Personal information can be hard to keep private on the Internet.

- Websites may ask for a name and date of birth to set up an account.
- Social media encourages users to share photos, job details, etc.
- Cloud services store personal files on their servers.

Privacy agreements say what a company can do with your information. You have to accept before using their service.

Privacy settings can sometimes be changed to make data more private. They're often fairly relaxed by default.

Users must trust companies to keep their data secure from leaks or theft.
Some privacy agreements allow your personal data to be sold to other companies.

Censorship and Surveillance

CENSORSHIP — controlling what information people can access.

Three things countries and governments may restrict access to:

1. Illegal content or websites supporting criminal activity like drugs or hate speech.
2. Age restricted content like gambling or pornography.

3. Foreign websites or websites that are critical of the government.

SURVEILLANCE — monitoring what people are accessing on the Internet.

- Government intelligence agencies look for words or phrases related to illegal activities, e.g. terrorism.
- Internet Service Providers may keep records of websites visited by customers.

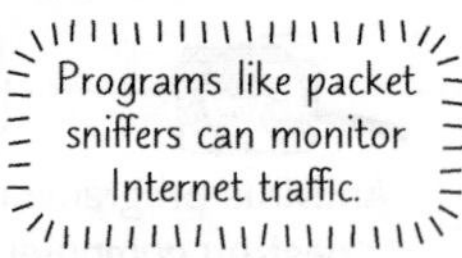

18+ Parents and schools also use parental-control software to filter content and monitor activity.

Anonymity

Online anonymity lets people be open and honest whilst protecting their identity.

Being anonymous online can also cause issues, particularly on social media:

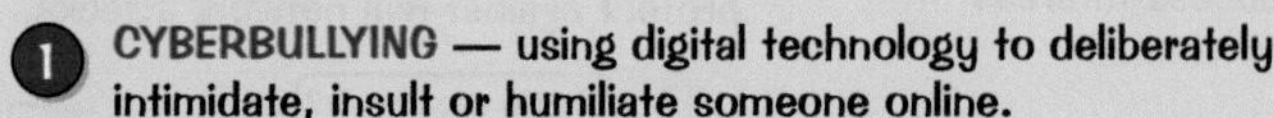

1. CYBERBULLYING — using digital technology to deliberately intimidate, insult or humiliate someone online.

2. TROLLING — making comments online to deliberately provoke an argument.

Cultural Issues and Wellbeing

Three Causes of the Digital Divide

DIGITAL DIVIDE — the inequality caused by unequal access to technology.

1. Devices and an Internet connection can be too expensive.
2. Urban areas often have greater network coverage than rural areas.
3. People may have difficulty adopting new technology — usually due to not being taught how to use it or not growing up with it.

There is a global divide due to different access to technology in different countries. Projects and charities have been set up to combat the digital and global divide.

Five Examples of Cultural Changes

1. Selfies — social media and smartphone cameras make sharing photos easy. This may make people more self-obsessed.
2. Viral videos — the Internet allows videos to rapidly spread. People and organisations try to use this for promotion.
3. Social media — allows people to publish writing, art and other media. Gives a voice to those ignored by mainstream media.
4. Streaming services allow people to listen to music and watch TV, often through a subscription service.
5. The sharing economy is driven by services in which people use new technology to make money from things they already own.

- Spare rooms rented to tourists.

- Cars used for taxi or delivery services.

Wellbeing and Health

Impacts on Social Wellbeing

- Smartphones make it easy for work to intrude into other areas of life. This can be stressful for employees.
- Face-to-face interactions can be neglected as social life and working life moves online.
- Companies regularly release new technology which people can feel pressured into buying.

Three tech-related health problems:

1. Eyestrain from looking at a screen for too long or too closely.

2. Repetitive strain injury caused by using devices for extended periods of time.

3. Back pain resulting from poor posture or bad seating.

Environmental Issues

Natural Resources

Electronic devices contain lots of raw materials.

Crude oil is used to make plastics for packaging, casing and other parts.

Precious metals are used in wiring and circuit boards.
E.g. gold, silver, copper, mercury, palladium, platinum and indium.

Non-renewable resources like coal, oil and gas are used to generate electricity.

Extracting these materials uses lots of energy, creates pollution (e.g. greenhouse gases) and depletes scarce resources.

Electricity Usage

Devices use a lot of energy in the form of electricity.

Computers and servers also generate heat. They are often cooled using fans or air-conditioned rooms which uses even more electricity.

There are ways to reduce electricity waste:

Problem	Solution
Desktops, laptops and smartphones are left idle.	Sleep and hibernate modes reduce power consumption.
Servers don't use all of their processing power.	Multiple virtual servers can run on one physical server.

E-Waste

Millions of electronic devices are discarded every year.

Three ways device manufacturers and retailers can contribute to this problem:

 1. Providing short warranties.

 2. Pricing — cheaper to replace than repair.

 3. Marketing to convince people to upgrade.

To cut costs, lots of e-waste is sent to countries where regulations are less strict. Most ends up in landfill and can be a hazard — toxic chemicals can leak into groundwater and harm wildlife.

The Waste Electric and Electronic Equipment (WEEE) directive covers:

- Disposing of e-waste safely.
- Promoting reuse, e.g. refurbishing broken devices.
- Recycling materials, e.g. extracting precious metals.

Legislation and Licensing

Six Principles of the Data Protection Act 2018

1. Data must be used in a fair, lawful and transparent way.
2. Data must be used for the specified purposes.
3. Data gathered should be relevant and not excessive.
4. Data must be accurate and kept up to date.
5. Data should not be kept longer than necessary.
6. Data should be kept safe and secure.

Data subjects have the right to see, amend and delete their personal data.

Organisations must register with the government before collecting personal data.

Copyright, Designs and Patents Act 1988

Copyright covers written or recorded content, e.g. videos, music, software.

Patents cover new inventions — they protect ideas and concepts.

All intellectual property is automatically protected, so it's illegal to use, copy and distribute material without the correct permission.

Copyright and patent holders can grant permission to use material for a fee.

Three Offences under the Computer Misuse Act 1990

Introduced to stop hacking and cyber crime.

1. Gaining unauthorised access to a private network or device.
2. Gaining unauthorised access in order to commit a crime.
3. Unauthorised modification of computer material.

An act of computer misuse (c. 1990)

Software Licensing

SOFTWARE LICENCE — a legal agreement stating how software can be used.

OPEN SOURCE SOFTWARE — source code made freely available.	
Pros	**Cons**
• Usually free • Can be legally adapted • Often innovative • Reliable and secure if popular	• Irregular updates if unpopular • Limited documentation • No warranties or support

PROPRIETARY SOFTWARE — only compiled code is available.	
Pros	**Cons**
• Warranties and support • Well-tested and documented • Usually regularly updated	• Often expensive • Can't legally be adapted • Old versions may not be supported

Computational Thinking & Pseudocode

Three Key Techniques for Computational Thinking

1.  **DECOMPOSITION — breaking down a complex problem into lots of smaller ones.**
2.  **ABSTRACTION — simplifying a problem by picking out the important bits of information.**
3.  **ALGORITHMIC THINKING — coming up with a series of logical steps to get from a problem to a solution.**

EXAMPLE

Find the quickest route by car between two places.

1. Decomposition: What is the length of each route?
   What are the speed limits on each route?
2. Abstraction:

Details to ignore	Details to focus on
Distance as the crow flies	Shortest route along the roads
Road names	Traffic information

3. Algorithmic thinking:
   1) List all potential routes.
   2) Find lengths of each route.
   3) Calculate time for each route.
   4) Find route with shortest time.

Pseudocode

ALGORITHM — a set of instructions for solving a problem.

PSEUDOCODE — a simple way of writing an algorithm without using a specific programming language.

There are no exact rules, but good pseudocode will be:
- **readable and easy to interpret**
- **not too vague**
- **structured like a piece of code**
- **easy to convert into any language**

EXAMPLE

Design an algorithm to filter items on a website so only those that cost £10 or less are shown.

```
n = number of items

for i = 1 to n
    itemPrice = cost of item i
    if itemPrice <= £10 then
        show item i
    else
        hide item i
    endif
next i
```

Loop goes through each item one by one.

Checks whether each item should be shown.

Flowcharts

Flowchart Symbols

Symbol	When It's Used	Symbol	When It's Used
Start / Stop	At the beginning and end of the algorithm	Decision	For a question — often a 'yes or no'
Inputs/Outputs	For values that are put in or taken out	Sub Program	To reference other flowcharts
Processes	E.g. for instructions and calculations	→	To connect boxes and show direction

Sequence

SEQUENCE — only has one route from start to stop.

Selection

SELECTION — has decisions which give multiple routes from start to stop.

Iteration

ITERATION — contains a loop that lets you repeat a task.

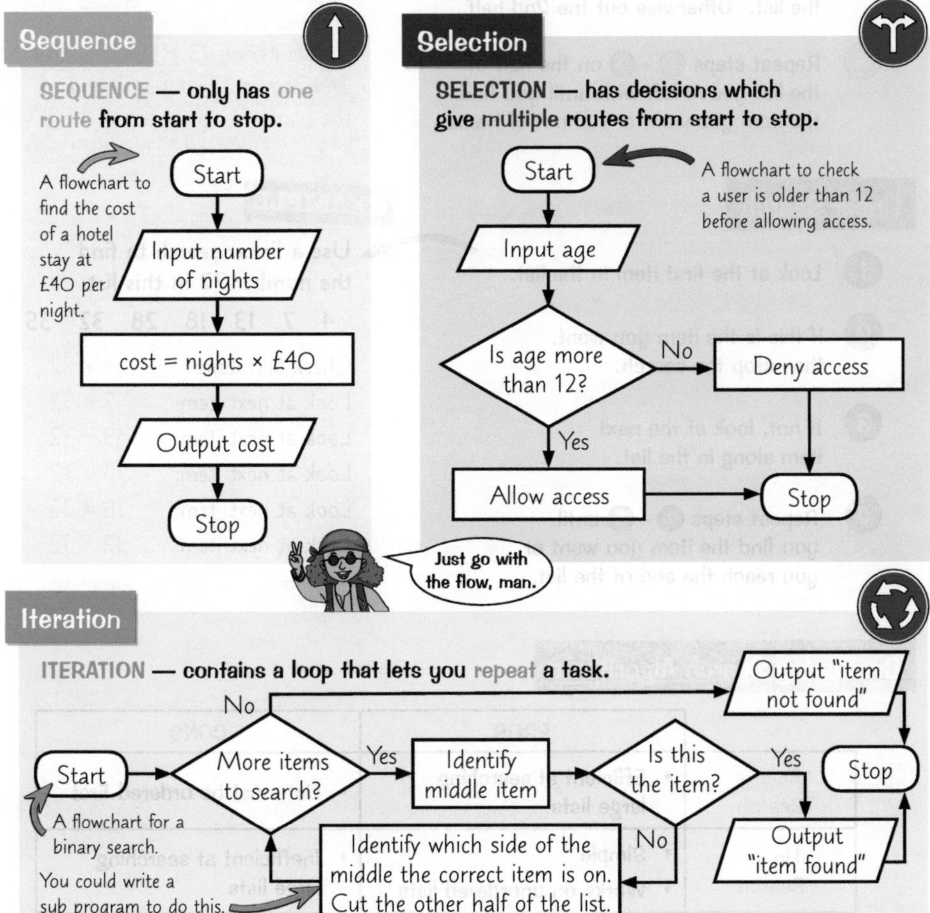

Search Algorithms

Binary Search

The list must be ordered.

1. Find the middle item — for n items, do $\frac{(n+1)}{2}$ and round up if needed.
2. If this is the item you want, then stop the search.
3. If not, compare the two items. If the item you want comes after the middle item, cut the 1st half of the list. Otherwise cut the 2nd half.
4. Repeat steps 1 - 3 on the half of the list you're left with until you find the item you want or run out of items.

EXAMPLE

Use a binary search to find the number 32 in this list:

4 7 13 18 28 32 35

There are 7 items,
middle item is (7 + 1) ÷ 2 = 4th.
4th item is 18 and 18 < 32 so cut first half of the list.

~~4 7 13 18~~ 28 32 35

There are 3 items left,
middle item is (3 + 1) ÷ 2 = 2nd
2nd item is 32 so item found, the search is complete.

Linear Search

1. Look at the first item in the list.
2. If this is the item you want, then stop the search.
3. If not, look at the next item along in the list.
4. Repeat steps 2 - 3 until you find the item you want or you reach the end of the list.

EXAMPLE

Use a linear search to find the number 32 in this list:

4 7 13 18 28 32 35

Check first item: 4 ≠ 32
Look at next item: 7 ≠ 32
Look at next item: 13 ≠ 32
Look at next item: 18 ≠ 32
Look at next item: 28 ≠ 32
Look at next item: 32 = 32
Item found — search complete.

Comparing Search Algorithms

	PROS	CONS
Binary Search	• Efficient at searching large lists	• List must be ordered first
Linear Search	• Simple • Works on unordered lists	• Inefficient at searching large lists

Bubble Sort and Insertion Sort

Bubble Sort

1. Look at the first two items in the list.
2. If they're in the right order, leave them. Otherwise, swap them.
3. Move on to the next pair of items (2nd and 3rd entries) and repeat step 2.
4. Repeat step 3 until you reach the end of the list — this is one pass. The last item is now in the correct place, so don't include it in the next pass.
5. Repeat steps 1 - 4 until there are no swaps in a pass.

EXAMPLE

Use a bubble sort to write these letters in alphabetical order:

C A K E

The algorithm is only complete when there are no swaps in a pass.

1st pass:	C	A	K	E	Compare C and A – swap them.
	A	C	K	E	Compare C and K – leave them.
	A	C	K	E	Compare K and E – swap them.
	A	C	E	K	End of first pass.
2nd pass:	A	C	E	K	Compare A and C – leave them.
	A	C	E	K	Compare C and E – leave them.
	A	C	E	K	No swaps so the list is sorted.

Insertion Sort

1. Look at the second item in the list.
2. Compare it to all items before it and insert the item into the right place.
3. Repeat step 2 for each remaining item until the last item in the list has been inserted in the correct place.

EXAMPLE

Use an insertion sort to order these numbers from smallest to largest:

6 2 7 3 1 4

6	2	7	3	1	4	Insert 2 before 6.
2	6	7	3	1	4	No insertion.
2	6	7	3	1	4	Insert 3 between 2 and 6.
2	3	6	7	1	4	Insert 1 before 2.
1	2	3	6	7	4	Insert 4 between 3 and 6.
1	2	3	4	6	7	Last item inserted, so the list is sorted.

Merge Sort

Merge Sort

1. Split the list into two sub-lists — start the second sub-list at the middle item.
2. Repeat step 1 on each sub-list until all sub-lists only contain one item.
3. Merge pairs of sub-lists back together. Each time you merge two sub-lists, sort the items into the right order.
4. Repeat step 3 until you've merged all the sub-lists together.

Merge sorts are efficient for computers because:

- Smaller lists are easier to sort.
- It's quick to merge ordered lists.

EXAMPLE

Use a merge sort to order these numbers from largest to smallest.

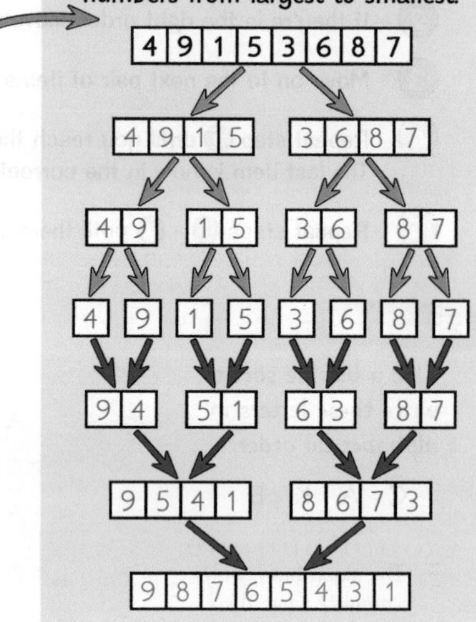

Comparing Sorting Algorithms

	PROS	CONS
Bubble Sort and Insertion Sort	• Simple and easy to implement • Quick to check if a list is already sorted • Doesn't need much memory, sorting only uses original list	• Inefficient on large lists
Merge Sort	• Efficient on large lists • Running time unaffected by order of items in original list	• Slower on small lists • Goes through whole process even if list is already sorted • Uses more memory in order to create sub-lists

Data Types & Random Numbers

Five Basic Data Types

1 INTEGER
- Whole numbers
- E.g. 0, –35, 1254

2 REAL/FLOAT
- Decimal numbers
- E.g. 3.14, –150.2

3 BOOLEAN
- Two values
- E.g. True/False, 1/0, yes/no

4 CHARACTER
- One letter, digit or symbol
- E.g. "X", "5", "?", "#"

5 STRING
- Text — a collection of characters
- E.g. "Xm2Pe5", "@cgpbooks.co.uk"

Casting

Functions can convert between data types...

- `int("5")` ← String "5" to integer 5
- `real(3)` or `float(3)` ← Integer 3 to decimal 3.0
- `str(123)` ← Integer 123 to string "123"
- `bool(0)` ← Integer 0 to Boolean False

... and between characters and ASCII numbers.

- `ASC("A")` ← Character 'A' to integer 65
- `CHR(65)` ← Integer 65 to character 'A'

Choosing Data Types

Using correct data types makes code more:

1. **Memory efficient**
2. **Robust**
3. **Predictable**

Using the wrong data type could mean your code gives errors or unexpected results.

Random Number Generation

Generate random numbers by using this function. → `random(x, y)`

x and y can be integers or reals.

- `random(10, 99)` ← A random integer between 10 and 99 (including 10 and 99).
- `random(3.0, 7.0)` ← A random real number between 3.0 and 7.0 (including 3.0 and 7.0).

Random numbers can be used to make unknown things happen in your program. E.g. to make choices and set attributes randomly.

Operators

Arithmetic Operators

Perform maths functions on two integer or real values.

Operator	Function	Example	Result
+	**Addition**	4 + 5	9
–	**Subtraction**	6 - 9	-3
*	**Multiplication**	3 * 8	24
/	**Division**	35 / 5	7
^	**Exponentiation**	2^3	8
DIV	**Quotient**	19 DIV 4	4
MOD	**Remainder**	19 MOD 4	3

BODMAS is used to evaluate expressions, so 9 – 6/3 gives 9 – 2 = 7.

DIV gives the whole number part of a division.

MOD gives the remainder of a division.

Comparison Operators

Compare two expressions and return a Boolean value (True or False).

Operator	Meaning	Returns True	Returns False
==	**is equal to**	"A" == "A"	"A" == "B"
!=	**is not equal to**	6.5 != 7.0	7 != 7
<	**is less than**	8 < 9	6.5 < 6.5
>	**is greater than**	10 > 9	12 > 13
<=	**is less than or equal to**	6 <= 6	6 <= 5
>=	**is greater than or equal to**	1 >= 0	2 - 3 >= 0

Comparison operators are checked after other operators are performed.

Boolean Operators

Work with Boolean values/expressions and return True or False.

Operator	How it Works	Returns True	Returns False
NOT	**Returns True when the expression is False.**	NOT(6 < 5)	NOT(4 <= 5)
AND	**Returns True when both expressions are True.**	1 <= 1 AND 2 == 2	7 > 5 AND 0 < 1
OR	**Returns True when either expression is True.**	2 > 5 OR 3 < 6	4 >= 8 OR 6 == 9

Order of operations: brackets, NOT, AND then OR.

Boolean Logic

Three Types of Logic Gates

Logic gates are special circuits built into computer chips.
They receive binary data, apply a Boolean operation, then output a binary result.

1 NOT — Input → NOT gate symbol → Output

Input	Output
0	1
1	0

2 AND — Input A, Input B → AND gate symbol → Output

Input A	Input B	Output
0	0	0
0	1	0
1	0	0
1	1	1

3 OR — Input A, Input B → OR gate symbol → Output

Input A	Input B	Output
0	0	0
0	1	1
1	0	1
1	1	1

Combining Logic Gates

Logic gates can be combined into circuits.
For example, AND followed by NOT:

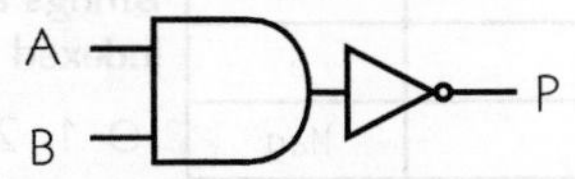

Written as P = NOT (A AND B)

Operations in brackets are done first.

A	B	A AND B	NOT (A AND B)
0	0	0	1
0	1	0	1
1	0	0	1
1	1	1	0

Two-Level Logic Circuits

Two-level means each input passes through at most two gates.

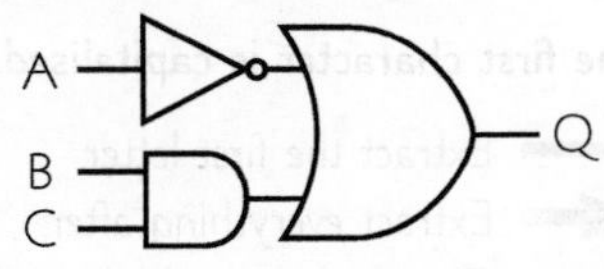

Written as Q = (NOT A) OR (B AND C)

Short Boolean algebra notation.

A	B	C	$\neg A$	$B \wedge C$	$Q = \neg A \vee (B \wedge C)$
0	0	0	1	0	1
⋮	⋮	⋮	⋮	⋮	⋮
1	1	0	0	0	0
1	1	1	0	1	1

Full truth table has $2^3 = 8$ rows as there are 3 inputs.

Variables and Strings

Storing Data Values

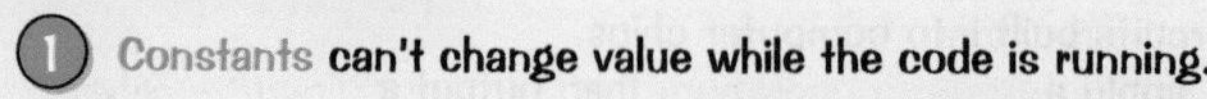

1. Constants can't change value while the code is running.

```
const daysInWeek = 7
```

2. Variables can change value.

```
length = 3
length = length * 10
```

The assignment operator (=) assigns values.

- Variable name (identifier) on the left.
- Value or expression on the right.
- Stored data values can be accessed later in a program.

Inputs and Outputs

Use input() to get data from a user.

```
name = input("Enter name:")
```

Use print() to display data to a user.

```
print("An error occurred.")
```

Put a string here to display it to the user.

Manipulating Strings

Strings are usually written in double quotes.
Use the + operator to concatenate (join) strings.

```
str = "pear"
print("Ugh, my " + str + " is about to reap" + str)
```

Function	Returns	Example (s = "Magic")	Result
upper	Upper case	s.upper	MAGIC
lower	Lower case	s.lower	magic
length	No. of characters	s.length	5
left(n)	First n characters	s.left(3)	Mag
right(n)	Last n characters	s.right(2)	ic
substring(a, b)	String starting at index a, length b	s.substring(1,3)	agi

Strings are indexed from 0:

0	1	2	3	4
M	a	g	i	c

'a' has index (position) 1.

EXAMPLE

Reformat the variable 'name' so that only the first character is capitalised.

```
first = name.left(1)
rest = name.right(name.length - 1)
name = first.upper + rest.lower
```

- first = name.left(1) — Extract the first letter.
- rest = name.right(name.length - 1) — Extract everything after.
- name = first.upper + rest.lower — Change case and join.

Selection

IF Statements

Check if a condition is True or False before running code. IF statements start with 'if [condition] then' and end with 'endif'. The 'else' part is optional.

Start
Condition True?
Yes — Run code under 'then'
No — Run code under 'else'
Stop

EXAMPLE

Code indented under 'then' is run when the condition is True.

```
if tickets > 0 then
    print("Tickets available.")
else
    print("Sorry, sold out!")
endif
```

Code indented under 'else' is run when the condition is False.

IF-ELSEIF Statements

Check different conditions and run the code under the first one that is True.

EXAMPLE

```
if score > 90 then
    print("Amazing – well done!")
elseif score > 60 then
    print("Great effort!")
elseif score > 30 then
    print("Room for improvement!")
else
    print("Keep practising!")
endif
```

What to do if ...

...first condition is True.

...first condition is False, second condition is True.

...first and second conditions are False, third condition is True.

...all conditions is False.

IF
ELSE

SWITCH Statements

Check if a variable has specific values before running code.

EXAMPLE

The value of 'answer' determines which case to use.

Each case should be indented to the same place.

```
answer = input("What is 5 - 7?")
switch answer:
    case -2:
        print("Correct!")
    case 2:
        print("Forgot minus sign?")
    default:
        print("Wrong!")
endswitch
```

Don't forget colons.

Default case comes at the end and used if no other case is correct.

SWITCH only checks a single variable, not multiple conditions like IF-ELSEIF.

Iteration

FOR Loops

Repeat code a fixed number of times. Number of repeats depends on initial value, end value, and step count (optional).

FOR loops are count-controlled.

Code to repeat is indented between 'for' and 'next'.

```
for k = 1 to 15 step 2
    print(k)
next k
```

Counts up in steps of 2. Default step count is 1.

The counter variable can be used inside the loop.

DO UNTIL Loops

Repeats until a condition is True.

Condition checked at end of loop.

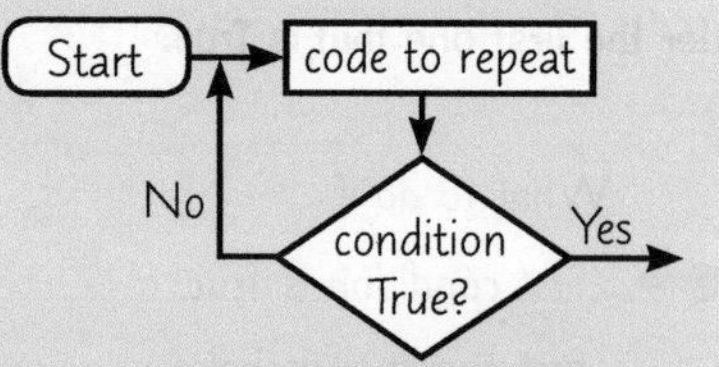

Always runs code at least once.

Infinite loop if condition always False.

These two loops are condition-controlled.

WHILE Loops

Repeats while a condition is True.

Condition checked at start of loop.

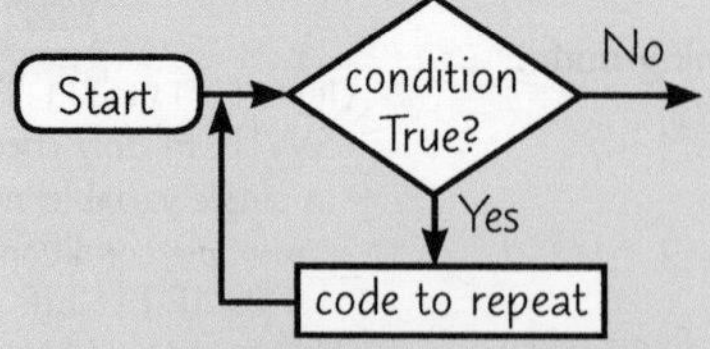

Never runs code if condition is False.

Infinite loop if condition always True.

LOOP-THE Loops

Repeat until queasy.

EXAMPLE

Write code for a dart game that counts down from 301. Stop when the player reaches 0. If they go under 0, ask them to throw again.

Using DO UNTIL — code to repeat goes between 'do' and 'until'.

```
score = 301
do
    throw = input("Enter throw:")
    if score - throw < 0 then
        print("Throw again")
    else
        score = score - throw
    endif
    print(str(score) + " left")
until score == 0
```

Using WHILE — code to repeat goes between 'while' and 'endwhile'.

```
score = 301
while score != 0
    throw = input("Enter throw:")
    if score - throw < 0 then
        print("Throw again")
    else
        score = score - throw
    endif
    print(str(score) + " left")
endwhile
```

Checking Multiple Conditions

Nested Selection Statements

Make another selection depending on the outcome of a previous selection.

EXAMPLE

Write an algorithm that checks a user's age. If they're under 9, ask them to multiply their age by 7 and check their answer. Print a different message for each possible outcome.

```
age = input("How old are you?")
if age < 9 then
    answer = input("Multiply your age by 7:")
    if answer == age * 7 then
        print("That's correct!")
    else
        print("Learn the 7 times table.")
    endif
else
    print("You're too old for this test.")
endif
```

Indentation makes nested statements more readable.

There can be statements nested inside the 'if' part, the 'else' part, or both.

Using Boolean Operators

Come on Meg, think. What was it?

Boolean operators can be used in selection and iteration statements to check more than one condition at once.

EXAMPLE

Use a while loop to give 3 attempts to enter one of two valid passwords ("Meg123" or "Adm1n!"). Once a valid password is entered, set 'access' to True and exit the loop, otherwise 'access' should be False.

```
attempts = 0
access = False
while attempts < 3 AND access == False
    pw = input("Password:")
    attempts = attempts + 1
    if pw == "Meg123" OR pw == "Adm1n!" then
        access = True
    endif
endwhile
```

Repeat while fewer than 3 attempts have been made, and while 'access' is False.

Check both passwords in a single IF statement condition.

Arrays

Purpose of Arrays

ARRAY — a data structure that stores a collection of values with the same data type.

- **Each value is called an element.**
- **Elements are accessed by position (index), starting at position 0.**

One-Dimensional Arrays

A 1D array is like a list.

You can either create arrays by setting their size, then assigning values...

```
array friends[3]
friends[0] = "Abi"
friends[1] = "Ben"
friends[2] = "Cho"
```

Can contain 3 elements (at positions 0, 1 and 2).

... or do it in one step by giving initial values:

```
array friends = ["Abi", "Ben", "Cho"]
```

Retrieve elements by position.

```
print(friends[0])
```

```
Abi
```

Change elements by assigning new values.

```
friends[1] = "Bilal"
```

Replaces element at position 1 ("Ben") with "Bilal".

Two-Dimensional Arrays

A 2D array is like a table. You can also think of them as a 1D array where each element is a 1D array.

Positions of elements are written like [a, b] or [a][b].

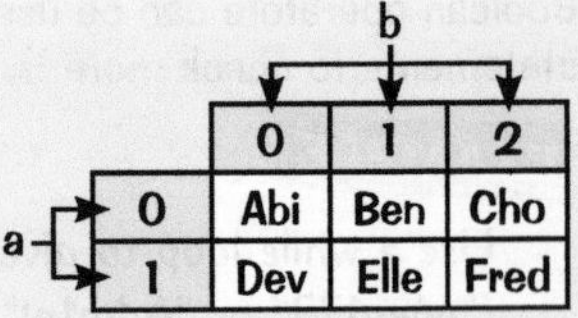

a \ b	0	1	2
0	Abi	Ben	Cho
1	Dev	Elle	Fred

EXAMPLE

The 2D array 'runs' is used to store the number of runs scored by two cricketers in their last four matches. E.g. runs[2, 0] returns 65.

Write an algorithm to set all values in the array back to 0.

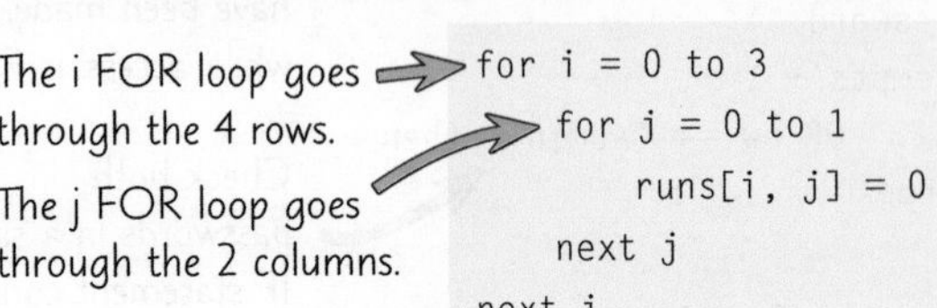


```
for i = 0 to 3
    for j = 0 to 1
        runs[i, j] = 0
    next j
next i
```

		Cricketer	
		0	1
Match	0	54	14
	1	83	22
	2	65	37
	3	58	26

File Handling

External Files

Allow programs to access data that's not written directly in the code.

Can store data so that it's not lost when a program is closed.

Six File Operations

1 `newFile("myFile.txt")`

Creates a new file with the given name (or path).

2 `file = open("myFile.txt")`

Opens a file — the file needs to be assigned to a variable.

These commands are called on the variable that stores the file.

3 `file.readLine()`

Returns the next line of the file, starting from the beginning.

After this command, the file 'cursor' moves to the beginning of the next line.

4 `file.writeLine("text")`

Writes a new line at the end of the file.

5 `file.endOfFile()`

Returns True if the 'cursor' is at the end of the file, otherwise False.

6 `file.close()`

Closes the file allowing other users to access the updated file.

EXAMPLE

Karim's shopping list is stored in an array called 'list'. The variable 'n' stores the number of items in the list.

```
list = ["eggs", "bread", "milk"]
n = 3
```

a) Write an algorithm to save the list to an external file.

```
filename = "shopping.txt"
newFile(filename)
shopList = open(filename)
for i = 0 to n - 1
    shopList.writeLine(list[i])
next i
shopList.close()
```

The file will look like this.

```
eggs
bread
milk
```

b) Write an algorithm to output every line from the file "stock.txt" so Karim can check which items the shop has.

```
stock = open("stock.txt")
while NOT stock.endOfFile()
    line = stock.readLine()
    print(line)
endwhile
stock.close()
```

Storing and Searching Data

Records

RECORD — a data structure that stores related values of different data types.

FIELD — an element of a record used to store one piece of data.

Create a fixed record structure by giving a data type and name for each field.

```
record ticket
    string filmName
    int seatNumber
    real price
endrecord
```

Create records by giving values for each field:

```
ticket1 = ticket("Data Force", 16, 7.50)
```

Use the variable and field name to access values:

```
print(ticket1.seatNumber)
```

→ 16

You can use arrays to group records with the same structure together.

SQL

Structured Query Language (SQL) is used to create, search, update and maintain database tables.

The columns are fields.

Each row is a record.

Table: cars

ID	regNum	year	price	fuel
1	JZ23 IQZ	2023	24000	Petrol
2	XJ18 QSI	2018	8999	Diesel
3	IQ21 UIK	2021	12500	Petrol

SELECT and FROM

Statements to specify which fields to return from which tables.

```
SELECT * FROM cars
```

Use this character to return all fields...

```
SELECT regNum FROM cars
```

...or list which field(s) to return from each record.

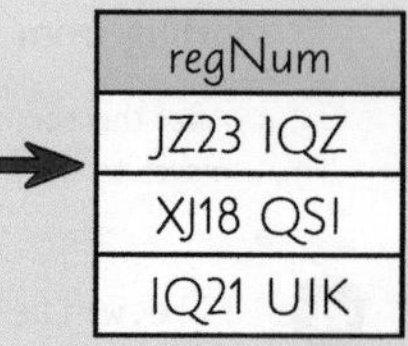

regNum
JZ23 IQZ
XJ18 QSI
IQ21 UIK

WHERE

A statement to specify conditions that a record should satisfy before being returned. Use Boolean operators to check multiple conditions.

EXAMPLE

Write a search query to return the year and price of all cars with price less than 20000 and fuel not equal to "Diesel".

```
SELECT year, price FROM cars
WHERE price < 20000 AND fuel != "Diesel"
```

year	price
2021	12500

Sub Programs

Key Definitions

SUB PROGRAM	**A set of instructions stored under one name that are executed when called. They help to improve code structure, improve readability and avoid repeating code.**
PARAMETER	**A variable used to pass data into a sub program. Can be any data type (e.g. integer, string, array, etc.).**
ARGUMENT	**The value a parameter takes when a sub program is called.**
LOCAL VARIABLE	**Can only be used within the structure they're declared in.**
GLOBAL VARIABLE	**Declared with the keyword 'global'. Can be used any time after declaration, in any part of the program.**

Procedures

PROCEDURE — a sub program that doesn't return a value.

Sub programs are declared with a name and parameters in brackets.

Call a procedure using its name. Give any arguments in brackets.

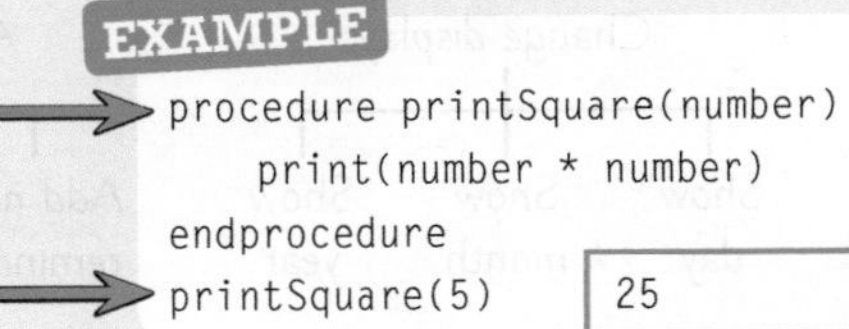

EXAMPLE

```
procedure printSquare(number)
    print(number * number)
endprocedure
printSquare(5)
```

```
25
```

Functions

FUNCTION — a sub program that does return a value.

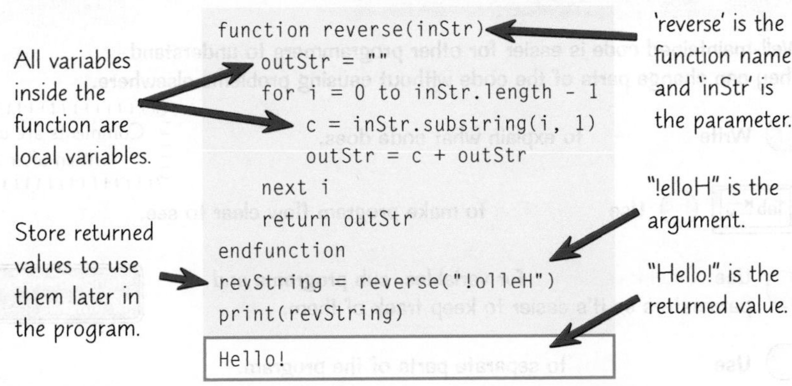

EXAMPLE

Write a function to reverse a string. Show it working on the string "!elloH".

```
function reverse(inStr)
    outStr = ""
    for i = 0 to inStr.length - 1
        c = inStr.substring(i, 1)
        outStr = c + outStr
    next i
    return outStr
endfunction
revString = reverse("!olleH")
print(revString)
```

```
Hello!
```

All variables inside the function are local variables.

Store returned values to use them later in the program.

'reverse' is the function name and 'inStr' is the parameter.

"!elloH" is the argument.

"Hello!" is the returned value.

Structured Programming

Using Structure Diagrams

STRUCTURE DIAGRAM — a tool you can use to help design and create programs.

1. Decompose the program into manageable modules.
2. Continue decomposing modules into smaller modules, until each one performs a simple task.
3. Write sub programs to carry out each task.
4. Build the bigger modules and main program from the sub programs.

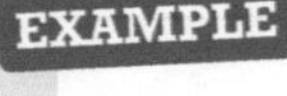

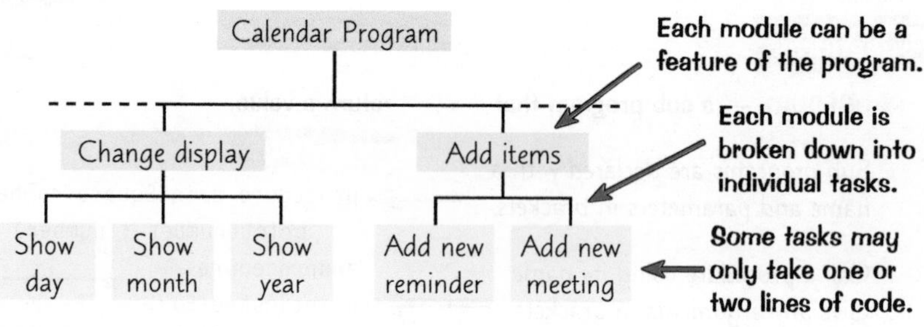

The advantage of using structure diagrams is that modules can be...

 Written independently  Tested individually  Reused elsewhere

Four Ways to Improve Maintainability

Well-maintained code is easier for other programmers to understand. They can change parts of the code without causing problems elsewhere.

1. Write comments to explain what code does.

Comments are usually written after //.

2. Use indentation to make program flow clear to see.
3. Use descriptive names for variables, sub programs and parameters so it's easier to keep track of them.

4. Use sub programs to separate parts of the program.

Defensive Design

Robust Programming

Programs that function correctly shouldn't break or produce errors.
Avoid these problems by using defensive design:

 Anticipate and prevent misuse by users.

 Keep code well-maintained.

 Reduce errors by testing.

Five Validation Checks

INPUT VALIDATION — checking if data meets certain criteria before passing it into a program.

Anne's presence check wasn't very conclusive.

Programs often use a mixture of validation checks, including:

Validation check	What it does...
1 Range check	Checks the data is within a specified range.
2 Presence check	Checks the data has actually been entered.
3 Format check	Checks the data has the correct format, e.g. a date.
4 Look-up table	Checks the data against a table of acceptable values.
5 Length check	Checks the data is the correct length.

Authentication

AUTHENTICATION — confirming the identity of a user before allowing access.
Passwords or biometrics are usually associated with a username.

Four ways to make passwords more secure:

1. Force strong passwords — long with a mix of letters, numbers and symbols.
2. Limit the number of failed authentication attempts.
3. Require that passwords are changed regularly.
4. Ask for a random selection of characters from a password on each attempt.

Errors and Trace Tables

Two Types of Error

1. **SYNTAX ERROR — when the rules or grammar of the programming language have been broken.**
2. **LOGIC ERROR — when a program is able to run, but does something unexpected.**

Translators can find syntax errors, but they won't pick up logic errors.

EXAMPLE

This function should check if a number is in a range.

Identify the syntax and logic errors.

```
function inRange(n, min, max
    if n > min OR n < max then
        return True
    else
        return False
    endif
endfunction
```

Syntax error: In line 1, there is a closing bracket missing at the end of the line.

Logic error: In line 2, the 'OR' operator won't always lead to the desired outcome — both conditions need to be true to get the correct result, so the 'AND' operator should be used there instead.

Trace Tables

Trace tables keep track of the value certain variables take as a program runs.

- **Columns usually represent variables.**
- **Rows show values of variables at a particular point.**

Columns could also represent other things, e.g. lengths of arrays.

They can be used to check for logic errors or to work out what a program is doing.

EXAMPLE

Complete the trace table when the algorithm below is run. Explain what the algorithm does.

```
a = 2
b = 3
c = 0
for i = 1 to b
    c = c + a
next i
print(c)
```

i	a	b	c	
—	2	3	0	← Values before the FOR loop.
1	2	3	2	← a is added to c each
2	2	3	4	← time i increases.
3	2	3	6	← Last value of c is output.

← Each variable has a column.

The algorithm calculates a × b and outputs the result.

Testing

Two Types of Testing

Testing can happen at different points in development:

ITERATIVE TESTING — testing a program while it's being developed.

- **Individual modules can be tested and errors fixed.**
- **Process is repeated until modules work correctly.**
- **Fixing small errors early prevents large errors later on.**

FINAL TESTING — testing a program at the end of development.

- **The whole program is tested at the same time.**
- **Check for errors where modules interact with each other.**

Final testing is sometimes called terminal testing.

Combining iterative and final testing helps minimise errors.

Four Types of Test Data

TEST PLAN — a detailed plan of how a program is going to be tested, including what test data will be used.

TEST DATA — inputs chosen to see if a program is working properly.

1. **NORMAL DATA — inputs users are likely to enter.**
2. **BOUNDARY DATA — values at the limit of what the program will accept.**
3. **INVALID DATA — has correct data type but should be rejected.**
4. **ERRONEOUS DATA — has incorrect data type and should be rejected.**

EXAMPLE

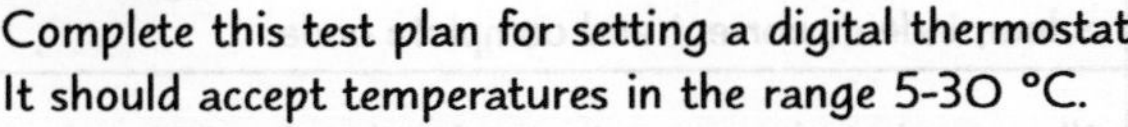
Complete this test plan for setting a digital thermostat.
It should accept temperatures in the range 5-30 °C.

Type	Test data	Reason for testing	Expected outcome
Normal	12	Check normal usage.	Temperature accepted
Boundary	30	Check the largest value.	Temperature accepted
Invalid	2	Check values that are too small.	Error: too small.
Erroneous	"1X"	Check non-numeric data.	Error: not recognised.

Languages, Translators & IDEs

High-Level Languages

The majority of code is written in high-level languages, e.g. Python.

- One instruction represents many instructions of machine code.
- Same code works on different machines and processors.
- Code is easy to read and write.
- Don't need to know about the processor or memory structure.
- Must be translated or interpreted before it can be executed.
- Slower and less memory efficient.

Low-Level Languages

Machine code ⟶ `00000 00010 00011...`
Assembly languages ⟶ `ADD r4, r2, r3`

- One instruction of assembly code can represent one of machine code.
- Code usually only works for one machine or processor.
- Code is hard to read and write.
- Need to know internal structure of CPU and how it manages memory.
- Machine code can be executed directly, without being translated.
- Faster and more memory efficient.

Two Types of Translator

1 COMPILER

- Translates all code at once into machine code, creating an executable file.
- Only needed for initial translation.
- Returns a list of errors for whole program when compiling is complete.
- Compiling can take a long time, but program runs quickly once compiled.

2 INTERPRETER

- Translates and runs one instruction at a time using its own machine code subroutines.
- Used every time code is run.
- Stops and returns first error found.
- Programs run more slowly.

Five Common Features of IDEs

INTEGRATED DEVELOPMENT ENVIRONMENT (IDE) — software to help develop programs.

Feature	Description
1 Code editor	Where code is written. Can often automatically colour, indent, correct and complete code.
2 Run-time environment	Allows code to be run and tested within the IDE.
3 Error diagnostics	Debugging tool to show information about detected errors.
4 Breakpoints	Pause the program at certain lines. Values can be checked to help diagnose logic errors.
5 Translator	A compiler or interpreter to allow source code to be executed.

CON041